P9-DOG-918

*Also by Kathy Mandry*

How to Make Elephant Bread
How to Grow a Jelly Glass Farm
The World on my Windowsill

# The First American Peanut Growing Book

# The First American Peanut Growing Book

Kathy Mandry

A Subsistence Press Book
Random House  New York

*Copyright © 1976 by Kathy Mandry and Subsistence Press, Inc.*

All rights reserved under International and Pan-American Copyright Conventions. Published in the United States by Random House, Inc., New York, and simultaneously in Canada by Random House of Canada Limited, Toronto.

Very special thanks to the Georgia Peanut Commission for information on growing peanuts at home; the Oklahoma Peanut Commission in Madill, Oklahoma, for the many recipes; the National Peanut Council and its Communication Division for the many pamphlets, recipes and information on peanut history and lore; the United States Department of Agriculture for peanut information.

Grateful acknowledgment is made to Little, Brown and Company for permission to reprint the recipe for Peanut Butter Soufflé on page 55 from *The Gourmet Peanut Butter Cook Book*, by Annabelle Simon. Copyright © 1975 by Annabelle S. Cahn.

*Library of Congress Catalog Card number: 76-43339*

*ISBN 0-394-41151-X*
*ISBN 0-394-73323-1 (pbk.)*

*Manufactured in the United States of America*
*9 8 7 6 5 4 3 2*
*First Edition*

*Plant drawings: Barbara Fiore. Divider drawings: Bill Plympton.*

Design: Samuel N. Antupit

To the biggest nut of all.

In America, we eat peanuts at the rate of eight pounds per person each year, mostly in an estimated ten trillion four hundred million peanut butter sandwiches. But it wasn't always this way. Not until the Civil War was over, the circus came to town, and baseball became a national obsession, did our national appetite for peanuts really start to grow!

Right now, 1.6 million acres of peanuts are growing in the United States alone. The state of Georgia, with 525,000 peanut acres, not only produces more than a third of our entire crop, but harbors our biggest peanut growing celebrity, Jimmy Carter! Even if you don't ever want to be President, you too can be a peanut farmer. Right in the privacy of your own home.

With as little as one raw peanut, some soil, a pot and a sunny spot, you can actually grow this strange little plant that ripens its peanut pods under the ground. Within five months you will be the amazed harvestor of your own peanut crop. It's easy, it's fun, and who knows what it could lead to?

## TYPES AND VARIETIES OF PEANUTS IN THE UNITED STATES *

*Virginia*

The Virginia-type varieties are large-podded and usually contain two seeds, which are relatively large and covered with a light reddish skin. There are several varieties of the Virginia group, all of which lose their identity when they reach the mill and become known merely as Virginias. The Virginia-type varieties are grown mainly in southeastern Virginia and northeastern North Carolina and to a lesser extent in Georgia and a few other locations where conditions

* from the United States Department of Agriculture

are suitable. Mostly used for cocktail peanuts and for roasting fancy peanuts in the hull. Some, though few, are used to make peanut butter.

## Runner

The Runner varieties are typically two-seeded. The pods may be cylindrical, with little constriction between the seeds. The skin covering the kernel is a light reddish brown. They are grown commercially in Alabama, Florida, and Georgia. There are many variety groups, commonly known as Dixie Runner, Alabama Runner, Georgia Runner, Carolina Runner, Wilmington Runner, Florunner. Mostly used to make peanut butter, oil and salted nuts.

## Spanish

The Spanish-type peanuts are generally two-seeded, small, and usually constricted between the seeds. The kernels are small and almost round. The skin covering the kernels is a pinkish tan, later turning to a light tan. Spanish-type peanuts are the most widely distributed type, grown chiefly in the Southeast and Southwest, mostly in Texas and Oklahoma. Used mainly in candy, confections, and to some extent, peanut butter and salted nuts.

## Valencia

The Valencia-type is mostly three-seeded and smooth, with no constriction of the pods. The kernels are very large. It is the most important of the unclassified varieties and is grown chiefly in New Mexico. Mostly these are roasted in the shell peanuts or "ball park peanuts" and sold in small packages at sporting events, country fairs, and circuses.

# Part 1

# Planting and Growing

# Chapter 1

When you crack open a peanut shell, the nuts inside, the very same nuts you would usually eat, are your seeds! But the seeds you start with to grow your peanut plant must be raw, not roasted. If the nuts are roasted, they won't ever sprout.

Tracking down raw peanuts should be fairly easy, the surest bet being a health food store. Gourmet shops, the kinds that sell fresh coffee beans from burlap sacks on the floor, often have raw peanuts, too. But here's a small catch. Four different kinds of peanuts are grown in this country: Spanish, Virginia, Valencia, and Runner. Since the types aren't marked on commercial packages, you won't know which ones you're getting. Now this really doesn't matter unless you happen to end up with the Runner type. Instead of growing a neat compact bush like the others, it grows as a vine and really needs to spread out. It'll need considerably more room than the 12-inch pot recommended for the others. Certainly, if you see your plant running, you can always cut it back, or transplant it into a bigger container. So, now that you know what chances you'll be taking, you can still take them. But, if you want to be sure of what you're getting, go to a garden store.

Garden stores sell peanut seeds in small labeled peanut called "Chico" because it takes the shortest packets. For the most fun, try using a Spanish type of amount of time to mature, 90 to 95 days, of any known peanut, whereas Virginia and Runner types can take up to 150 days.

If by any chance your local garden center doesn't have any peanut seeds, the H.G. Hastings Company in Atlanta, Georgia, will be happy to send you some. This year they have only the Valencia type for sale. Their supply depends on what's available. Peanut farmers need good seed to grow the next year's peanut crop. The seed comes from growers who grow nothing but "seed peanuts." So, for instance, if the Spanish "seed peanut" harvest is smaller than usual one year, and the farmers have no Spanish seeds to spare, Hastings won't have any. Next year they might have just Spanish and no Valencias. It all depends. But all seeds Hastings sells are approved by the state's Department of Agriculture so they're in good shape for germination. The price of the seeds? That varies year to year too, depending on the supply. Hastings puts out a catalog around the first of each year that they will send you free of charge. For the catalog or for seeds, write to H.G. Hastings Co., P.O. Box 4655, Atlanta, Georgia, 30302 or, telephone (404) 321-6981.

If you're feeling expansive, and you'd like to try planting Runners, do it. You can get Runners from Southern Roasted Nuts, Inc., P.O. Box 222, Damascus, Georgia, 31741. A 5-pound box, the smallest they have, is $2.70 this year (plus postage and shipping charges). For your Runners, you'll need a planter at least 24 inches long and 12 inches deep. Their branches could get to be two feet long and will lie close to the soil. For an ornamental plant, the Runner is the prettiest. It would look terrific in a hanging pot.

# Chapter 2

Now that you have your raw peanut. crack the shell open, gently, being very careful not to damage the red skin around the seeds. Take the seeds out and set them down. Don't throw away the shell, crush it and feed it to one of your houseplants. Peanut shells are great soil enrichers. The next step is soaking.

*The First Crack*

Your peanut plant will start to germinate faster if you soak your seeds overnight first. It gives them a head start. Just put them in any kind of small bowl filled with water. Use only tepid, or room temperature, water. Peanut seeds take in a great deal of water when they're germinating and can easily get sick if it's shocking cold water. All through the germination process and even when your peanut plant gets bigger, remember to avoid extremes of cold and hot.

*The Overnight Soak*

The sprouting of the seed, the growing from seed to seedling, is called germination. After their overnight bath, your seeds are ready to start germinating. There are a few methods to choose from. You can start your seed right away in a pot of soil and you won't ever need to move it from the pot unless you want to transplant it into the ground later. So, in a way, this is the least fuss. The drawback of this method is, for the first few days, all of the exciting first signs of growth

*Germination*

3.

Seed between
the paper and
the glass one
inch below the
rim.

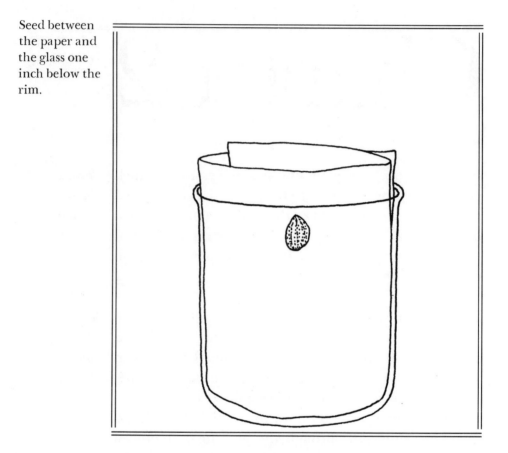

will be happening under the soil where you can't see
them. Two other methods, the Glass Method and the
Plastic Container Method, are more fun because you
can see what's happening. The first small root works
its way down, the side roots branch out, the seed splits
and opens up into two halves to let the young branches
and leaves surge out and upwards. You can let your
plant get to be 3 inches tall, watching it all the way,
before you put it in its pot.

*The Glass Method*   You'll need a glass or a jar, some
paper towels, and your peanut seeds, of course. Take
about three thicknesses of paper towels and roll them

into a cylinder just big enough to fit inside the glass. You can trim off any excess with scissors. Fill the glass with water until the paper towels are sopping wet. Let the glass stay about halfway filled with water. The seed needs to be kept moist so don't let the towels dry out. Again, remember to use tepid water, no extremes of hot or cold. Take your peanut seed and snuggle it in between the paper and the glass about one inch below the rim. If you're starting two seeds, you can snuggle the other one in on the other side of the glass, or even better, start it in its own glass. In just a few days, the root will show. This is the part of the plant that always

Ready for transplanting.

shows first so if the root is growing on the top of your seed, the seed is in the glass upside-down. You might want to gently turn it the other way so the root's growing down. Of course, eventually the peanut root will find its way down and the stem will find its way up to the light. It's one of those laws of nature. But why not make it a little easier? From 5 to 10 days after the root shows up, your peanut seedling should be growing above the rim of the glass. You can let it grow this way until it gets to be about 3 inches tall, then it's time to put it in a pot.

Root growth after a few days.

Stem growing out of split open seed.

*The Plastic Container Method* You'll need a small plastic container with a lid, several inches of thick yarn, any color is fine, and your peanut seeds. If you want to start both seeds, it's best to start each one in its own container. Both the lid and the bottom of the container must have a small hole poked in them. A see-through plastic container would be best, just because you could see through it better, but any kind of plastic will do. Put enough yarn in the container to fill the bottom. You can substitute paper towels, a piece of cloth, or any natural fiber that will retain moisture. Be wary of synthetics. Whatever you use, nestle the seed on its side in the middle of it all. Slowly water both seed and yarn, until the material is soaked and the water runs out the hole in the bottom. Again, tepid water, not too

Leaves devel-
oping along
the stem.

Ready for
transplanting.

cold or hot. Then put the lid on. Your seed needs to
be kept moist while germinating and the function of
the yarn is to retain moisture. Water the seed every
day. Keep the material sopping wet. Don't let the seed
dry out. In just a few days, a root should show up.
The seed will split open and the stem will appear.
When the root gets to be ½ inch long and the leaves
start growing, you can leave the lid off. Keep watering
daily. And try to keep any new roots covered with wet
material. You can let your peanut plant grow this way
until it's about 3 inches tall. Then it's time to put it
in a pot.

*The Right-in-the-Pot Method* The pot you put your peanut seeds in must be the same size and type you plan to grow the entire plant in, so it takes some planning. See the section on "Planting" for pot, gravel and soil requirements before you plant your seeds.

*The Planting* With this method, you'll have to plant 3 or 4 peanut seeds because you can only count on about 2 out of 3 or 4 germinating this way. Plant your peanut seeds 2 inches under the soil about 2 inches apart. The way you put them in makes no difference. In peanut fields they usually fall in on their sides. But even if you put them in upside-down, the root will still grow down and the stem will still grow up to the light. In about 5 to 10 days, your peanut seedlings should begin to poke through the soil surface. The actual time it takes will depend on your soil texture, how deep the seeds are planted, and the temperature. Be sure you continue to keep the soil moist.

*The Weeding Out* When your plants get to be about 2 weeks old, you'll have to decide which plant to keep. You can only grow one peanut plant to a pot, so you'll want to keep the most vigorous plant. You can tell which one that is just by looking. It'll be taller, bigger, and bushier than the others. To weed out the weaker ones, just place your fingers firmly around the plants, pressing your other hand against the surface of the soil, and pull them out. Then firm the soil around the remaining plant. If you were lucky, all your seeds made it, and each little plant looks pretty spunky to you, or if you can't find it in your heart to give up on the weaklings, you can always put the other plants in their own pots. Or you could try putting one in a smaller 4- to 5-inch pot just to get flowers. But you won't get peanuts in a small pot.

# Chapter 3

Trans-
planting
Seedlings
from a
Glass or
Plastic
Container
into
a Pot

*When to Pot*   When your peanut seedling grows to be about 3 inches tall, it's time to put it in a pot.

*The Pot Itself*   You'll need a pot 12 inches wide and 12 to 18 inches deep with a drainage hole and some kind of drainage saucer. Whether the pot is clay or plastic doesn't really matter but it should be big enough to accommodate the dense and profuse root system your plant will make. If you use a smaller pot, don't expect peanuts. The larger the pot, the more room for peanuts. If you want a really impressive yield of peanuts, you can plant a Runner in a large window-box. If you'd like to watch your peanuts developing under the ground, consider putting your plant in an aquarium. This could be fun.

*Gravel in the Pot*   Some gravel in the bottom of your pot, about ½ inch deep, might be very beneficial to your peanut plant. As your plant sends out its dense root system, it will displace more and more of the soil and cause it to pack in tighter. The gravel will aid in the very important function of drainage.

*The Soil*   A loose, friable (easily crumbled), sandy-textured soil is best. Peanut plants need a slightly acid soil that has been well fertilized. And since peanuts are especially susceptible to soil-borne organisms, the soil should be clean.

*Store-Bought Soil*   You can buy packaged,

After trans-
planting.

sterilized, potting soil in a garden store or plant store. Mix it with ⅓ sand. Not beach sand, the salt in that will kill your plant, but coarse sand for planting. You'll find it in the same place you'll find your potting soil.

*Garden Soil* If you have a good garden, use the soil from it. Peanuts function absolutely the best in soil already fertilized and with minerals already in it. You can tell if your garden soil has too much clay in it if the soil balls up into a lump when you rub it in your hands. To fix this, add about ⅓ sand to ⅔ soil. Again, not beach sand. Put this mixture right into your pot. *How to Pot* Dig a hole a few inches deep in the center of the pot and fill it with water. Place your seedling roots in the hole. The tops of the open seed should be just at the surface of the soil. Holding the seedling with one hand to keep it straight, sprinkle soil into the hole until a thin mud surrounds the roots. The plant should be able to stand up securely and not look or feel like it's going to shift position. Do not pack soil. If the soil settles, add more. Now find the plant a warm, sunny spot. You might want to shield the adjusting roots and seedling from direct sunlight for the next few days.

*Seedlings and Light* You don't need sunlight for your peanut seed to germinate. It will begin to grow even on a windowless kitchen counter. But as soon as your seed halves split apart and the seedling begins to emerge up from them, your plant definitely needs light. In your seed, the seed leaf, or cotyledon, which is really the first pair of leaves in the embryo, gives its stored food to the plant until the plant gets big enough to make its own food by photosynthesis. So when that seedling begins to emerge, it's big enough. To make

*12.*

food, it needs light. At this point, be sure it's in the sunniest spot you can find. However, going right from a shady spot to blazing hot sunlight can be an adjustment too big for your seedling to make. That can kill it. So be sure to shield seedlings from bright sunlight with a piece of cardboard for the first few days. Then take the cardboard away. Probably the best way to start your plant is in direct sunlight right from the very beginning, from the germination of the seed. That way your plant will need no acclimatizing process at all.

*When to Plant* You can transfer your plant outside to a good sunny spot in your garden anytime from the time it's 3 inches tall to the time it's 30 days old. This is accomplished with much less shock to the younger peanut plant under 30 days than to a plant 45 to 55 days old which is in blossom, or to a plant 60 to 90 days old which is already beginning to develop pods. Your peanut plant definitely has a better chance of making it outside if you put it there when it's still small. Be sure the soil is warm and there is no danger of frost.

*How to Plant* The procedure for planting outdoors is the same as planting in a pot. Read the section, "How to Pot."

*Planting Peanuts Outside in the Ground*

# Chapter 4

The Growth Chart is really very general. If your plant isn't exactly on schedule, don't worry. A lot depends on growing conditions, soil texture, temperature. If fruiting (pod development) isn't heavy, and it's not likely to be in your pot, vegetative growth will probably go on longer and at a more rapid rate. On a peanut farm, under the best growing conditions, the plant uses much energy to develop pods under the ground. But in a pot, under less than best conditions, the plant may very well use its energy to grow bigger and bushier. Though you may get less peanuts, you'll probably have a lusher plant than professional peanut growers ever see.

# DAY-TO-DAY
# PEANUT
# PLANT GROWTH
# CHART

| *What Happens Next?* | *Days Old* |
|---|---|
| As they take in water, the cells begin to enlarge and the seed swells. | 1–5 |
| The two meaty seed halves, or cotyledons, are providing rich stores of food for the young plant. | |
| The tip of the primary root breaks through the seed coat and starts growing down. | |
| The primary root continues to grow and lateral roots appear. | |
| The primary root can get to be 6 inches long. | |
| When planted in soil, the hypocotyl, that portion of the stem below the cotyledon and above the root, elongates, pushing the seed to the soil surface. It should crack the soil surface in about eight days. | |
| When started in a glass or plastic container, the seed splits open, and the stem and leaf bud grow up from the cotyledon or seed leaf. When the stem gets to be 3 inches tall, it's time to transplant. | |
| Plant is now nearly 3 inches tall. Leaves appear. Each leaf consists of a slender stem, or petiole, with 4 leaflets. | 5–10 |
| As soon as the leaves open the plant starts making its own food by photosynthesis. | |
| The crown of the plant will have a small cluster of leaflets, still folded, from which new shoot growth will happen. | 10–14 |
| Lateral branches begin developing. They are the origin of later flowering branches. Take care not to injure or bury them. | |

| | |
|---|---|
| 14–45 | Rapid vegetative growth.<br>Plant invests its energy in developing leaves and a strong underground root system for taking in nutrition and moisture from the soil. |
| 45–55 | Enzymes within the plant suddenly shift emphasis from vegetative growth to reproductive growth.<br>Pretty yellow flower buds develop.<br>Flower stalk appears.<br>The plant now flowers and continues to bloom for 8 more weeks. |
| 45 or 55–100 | Plant still blooming.<br>Some of the flowers that have already withered have developed pegs which curve downward, pulled by gravity, into the soil. At the tip of each peg is the peanut embryo which will develop into a pod.<br>By now the pegs have penetrated the soil. They continue to grow down until they're 2 to 3 inches deep. Then the tip of the peg, where the embryo is, gets bigger, turns horizontal, and pods begin to form.<br>Vegetative growth continues and plant continues to increase in size.<br>The underground pods swell and begin to form the familiar oblong tan shape. |
| 100–150 or longer | Plant is now about 18 inches tall. Or a low growing lush viney Runner. |
| Spanish "Chico": 95<br>Other Spanish: 100–120<br>Virginias: 100–140<br>Valencias: 100–140<br>Runners: 140 plus | Pods are maturing.<br><br>As maturity approaches, leaves may turn yellowish-green, indicating that the pods and nuts inside them have been taking the plant's food supply for their own growth.<br><br>Peanut pods, 15 to 20 of them, are mature under the soil and ready to be harvested.<br><br>In each pod are two seeds or nuts which can be eaten, or planted again as seed to grow more peanuts. |

*16.*

# Chapter 5

*Watering*  How much and how often you water your    *Water*
plant really depends on your soil texture and your pre-
vailing environment. The peanut plant must be kept
turgid, which means, literally, swollen or bloated.
When your seedling first goes into the soil, give it a
good watering. Water until the water starts to trickle
out the bottom of the pot. A rule of thumb is to thoroughly saturate the soil with water in this fashion every
3rd or 4th day. But if your plant seems to be wilting,
water it more often. Poke your finger under the soil. If
it feels dry, water it. But, don't overwater. The leaves
turn yellow from overwatering.

     The root system of your plant will grow rapidly.
And you'll probably find yourself having to water more
frequently as the root systems develop. Watering depends on your light and the amount of heat too. Trust
your instincts.

     The peanut plant is a spunky, hardy plant and
that's comforting to know. A friend of mine left his
small peanut seedling in its office-pot over a long holi-
day weekend. When he returned, all tanned and glow-
ing on a Tuesday morning, he was met by a drooped
over, very thirsty, very sad looking thing. It looked
like it had simply given up. Desperately, he watered it.
He had no high hopes. But just an hour later his gaze
was met by an erect, perked-up peanut plant all ready

to go on! And the plant's been none the worse for that weekend's neglect.

*Keep Its Feet Dry*  When the drainage saucer under your pot collects water, empty it. Don't let the water stand around in the saucer. Your peanut plant, in the words of one of our Georgia experts, doesn't like having "wet feet." That kind of wetness gives the roots and pods a chance to rot.

*Spraying the Leaves with Water*  Don't do it! Unless the humidity in your house is extremely low.

*Light*

*Sunlight*  The peanut plant is a tropical plant, a native of Peru, and needs sunlight. With 10 to 12 hours a day of full sunlight, it is growing under the best light conditions. It will grow on less light too, but you'll need a bare minimum of 5 hours of good sunlight a day. So put your plant in the sunniest window you have. If your plant doesn't have enough light, it'll grow up to be tall and skinny and just won't look pretty.

*Artificial Light*  If you don't have a good sunny window or a sunny spot outside, your plant can grow under strong fluorescent light. Though not as well. Our Georgia peanut expert said he had a lot of trouble raising peanuts in a greenhouse in the wintertime. He used artificial light. The plants grew, but just didn't look like those grown in the field under the summer sun. But in this case it might be fair to say that one man's failure can be another person's success!

*Your Plant Sleeps in the Dark*  All the leaves and leaflets on your plant will completely close in the dark. So the first time you see your plant all folded up at night, don't panic, it's only resting.

Peanut plants like to be warm. 85 to 95 degrees is best. *Temperature*
It will take much longer for peanut pods to develop
when your plant lives in 70- to 85-degree weather than
when it lives in 85- to 95-degree weather. The young
peanut plant won't do well in drafts so make sure your
window isn't letting any chilling drafts seep through.

To your potting soil-sand combination, you can add a *Fertilizing*
complete fertilizer. Commercially sold liquid mixes are
just fine. Follow instructions on your fertilizer or plant
food package. Thereafter, once or twice a month, you
can add some of the liquid mix to the water when you
water your plant. Be careful not to use too much
fertilizer, the most often you should ever feed it to your
plant is every two weeks.

Peanuts need their soil to be rich in calcium. If you're *Calcium*
using garden soil, it will most likely have some calcium *in the*
in it. If you're using a potting soil and sand mixture, *Soil*
it's a good idea to give your plant a booster of calcium
when the first peanut flowers start to bloom. You can
find calcium at a garden store. The more soluble the
calcium, the better. The most soluble of all is calcium
sulphate. Apply ½ ounce per 18-inch pot or per square
foot of soil to the surface, when the flowers start to
bloom. This is what the peanut farmers do. All you
need is a very, very small amount. If after reading
directions on the package, you're not sure about how
much to use, ask the people at your garden store. If
you don't have even the slightest leaning toward chem-
istry and the whole thing scares you, don't do it. Even
your potting soil probably has some calcium in it.
Adding the calcium will help your plant grow better
peanuts, but it's not really that crucial.

Insects and diseases are not likely to attack your peanut plant if it's growing in a pot. Outside, in your garden, it will be taking exactly the same chances your other plants have taken.

For the big peanut farmers, the most serious of peanut plant ailments is a disease called leaf spot that attacks foliage. Leaf spot not only makes the plant unsightly, it also greatly reduces its ability to grow and to yield peanuts. The first symptom of leaf spot is, you guessed it, a spot on the leaf. It will have a tannish brown center and be surrounded by a yellow halo. The lesion then continues to grow and spread. The disease usually starts on the lower leaves.

Leaf spot usually strikes those plants growing in soil that was used before to grow peanuts. So, don't worry, it's not likely to be a problem in your first peanut plant. But at least you know about it.

If your plant should develop leaf spot, use any fungicide available for the control of it, the same type of fungicide you'd use for leaf spot on a rose bush. Diamond Shamrock Chemical Co. makes one called Bravo.

# Chapter 6

Within 45 to 55 days after you start your seed, your plant will start to flower. Its small yellow flowers grow low on the plant and look just like the flowers of the sweet pea. Flowering will go on for about 8 weeks. Each flower will bloom for only 24 hours, then shrivel up. Leave the shrivelled flowers on your plant, don't pull them off. Let them fall off by themselves later. Flowering is an exciting time because now your plant is ready to start making peanuts.

*When the Flowers Come*

The purpose of the peanut flower, as with all flowers, is to make seeds. Each peanut flower comes equipped with both male and female reproductive parts. It is a self-sufficient flower. It fertilizes its own ovary located at the base of the flower stalk. Each flower fertilizes itself in about one day, then shrivels.

*How the Peanut Flower Makes Peanuts*

Within 5 to 10 days after the flower shrivels, the ovary begins to enlarge and extends into a stalk-like structure called a peg. The tip of the peg carries the immature peanut, the newly formed embryo. The peg, pulled by gravity, grows down towards the soil.

After it penetrates the soil surface, it continues to thrust down under the soil to a depth of 1 to 3 inches. Then the tips of the pegs begin to grow larger and turn horizontal. Now the tips start to develop into mature peanut pods. Do not disturb the pegs after they've penetrated the soil surface.

The first
flowering.

Full grown
plant in bloom.

Peg growing
toward the soil.

Peg

If your first peanut flower doesn't produce a peg, don't lose faith. You can't expect all of your flowers to produce pegs and pods. Less than 10 percent of the flowers on peanut farms actually produce mature peanuts. But if you take tender care of your plant for the next 60 to 80 days, it could reward you with 15 to 20 peanuts. Under the very best of conditions, a peanut plant is capable of producing up to 100 peanuts, with the average being around 45 or 50.

# Chapter 7

It takes from 60 to 80 days after the pegs have gone under the soil for them to ripen. Or, you can count from the time you started your seed. If you're growing the speedy "Chico" type of Spanish peanut, start looking at a pod in about 95 days from the day you soaked your seed overnight. For other types of Spanish, for Virginias and Valencias, look after 120 days. For Runners, look after 140 days.

*When to Start Testing for Ripeness*

This is the most difficult task in peanut farming and will be your most difficult task, too. How can you tell when your peanuts are ripe if they're under the soil? Here are some guidelines to follow:

*How Can You Tell When They're Ripe?*

      The hotter the climate, the faster you can expect your peanuts to mature.

      When the leaves of your peanut plant begin to show a pale yellowish-green color instead of their usual dark green color, the peanuts are ripe. The yellowish-green color indicates that the nuts have been using the plant's food supply for their own growth.

*Peanuts are ripe when . . .*
- . . . the nuts inside the pod show a deep rich pink color on the seed coat.
- . . . the inside of the pod turns dark and tiny veins show up on it.

25.

Peanuts ready
for harvest.

. . . the patterns of the pod are vaguely indented in the nut, as the peanuts become bigger and more packed in the pod.

Professional peanut farmers usually pull up several plants when it's near harvest time and check them out. Of course, they've got thousands of plants, but you've got your entire crop right there in one pot. So here's what to do. Gently burrow your fingers under the soil at the base of the stem. Keep burrowing until you locate, by feel, a peanut pod. Gently pull it up. If the pod snaps off the peg easily when you pull it up, that's a good sign that your nuts are ripe. Now, open the pod. If the nuts inside are watery and white to pink in color, wait about two weeks and try again. Trust your instincts. And don't lose faith now, you're nearly there. Don't worry. As long as your peanut plant is alive, growing, viable and in healthy condition, the peanuts won't rot so readily. So in pot harvesting, it's better to wait a little longer if you're in doubt than to rush it. Immature peanuts taste very bitter.

*How to Test for Ripeness*

    Here's something that you probably don't want to hear. Remember that all of your peanut flowers didn't bloom at the same time, so all of your peanuts will not be the same age. Some will be more mature than others. The idea is to harvest them when *most* of them are ripe. If this worries you, you can tag each peg with the date it started to go under the soil, keeping in mind that peanuts ripen in 60 to 80 days from the time that happens. Use soft yarn through a small piece of cardboard with a hole in it. Tag your peg high up so the paper tag doesn't end up mush after a few waterings.

If it's any consolation, peanut farmers have the same problem. If the plant is pulled up too early, the peanuts aren't good roasting quality. If they're pulled up too late, when they're too ripe, many of the peanuts break off from their pegs and just stay under the soil. A peanut farmer can lose a great deal of his crop like that. The peanut industry is constantly working on better techniques to determine ripeness.

*How to Harvest*

Loosen the soil around the main stem of your peanut plant with a potato fork or similar utensil. This will allow you to take your plant out of the soil more easily leaving the least number of pods still in the soil. After loosening, gently pull up the entire plant, roots and all. Gently shake your plant to get most of the soil off the pods and roots. To find peanuts left behind in the pot, burrow your hands around in the soil or dump everything out onto some newspapers. Rescue any peanut pods that might have gotten left behind. And listen, congratulations!

# Chapter 8

This is one of the most important operations in peanut harvesting. When dug, peanuts have 35 to 50 percent moisture which has to be reduced to 10 percent or less before they can be safely stored. And the way the peanuts are dried is important too. If dried too fast, they won't taste as good. If they're seed peanuts, the new peanut seeds will be less likely to germinate.

*The First Step*

Let your peanut plant sun dry out in the open for 4 or 5 days with the pods facing the sky, the leaves and stems facing the ground. They're best when dried outdoors, in the sunniest spot you can find. On peanut farms they are dried in rows in hot, sunny fields. If you can't dry them outside, a sunny windowsill is fine. Whatever, it should be a bright, light place.

*The Second Step*

After the 5th day, hand pick the pods from your plant and place them on a metal cookie sheet. Spread them out. Keep them in the sun like that until the peanuts inside the pods are completely dry of any detectable moisture. Just crack a pod open and take a look. Now you can decide what to do with your crop. You'll eat them, of course, the only thing in question is whether you want to eat them right away, or a little at a time. If you want to take your time, you can store them.

# Chapter 9

*Keep
an Eye on
Your
Peanuts*

If you store your peanuts right, you can keep them around for up to 12 months. According to our Georgia expert, absolutely the best way to store peanuts is to put them in a porous burlap bag and hang them up somewhere on your back porch. If you don't have such a thing, put them in any cool, dry, airy place where you can keep an eye on them. The top of a cupboard, or a closet you use a lot, so you don't forget about them, or something like that. The spot should be free from rodents and insects. There are insects that like seeds, and they can invade and destroy your harvest. Always store your peanuts in a porous bag or a paper bag that can be kept dry. Never in plastic bags. The peanuts will mold.

# Chapter 10

Actually, the peanut is a pea, not a nut at all, and belongs to the bean family. It is the pod or legume of Arachis hypogaea which has the strange habit of ripening under the ground. The pods, technically fruits because they contain seeds, ripen near the tap root of the plant.

*It's Not a Nut at All*

Also known as groundnut, goober, ground pea, guinea seed, pistache de terre, pindar, manilla nut, ground bean and monkey nut, the peanut has a growing season of from 95 to 175 days. It is an annual plant, ranging from an erect or bunch form (Spanish, Valencia, Virginia) 1½ to 2 feet high with short branches to a spreading or runner form (Runners) with branches up to 2 feet long that lie close to the soil. Stems and leaves are sturdy and hairy. Leaves are pinnated with two pairs of leaflets. Flowers are golden yellow and self-pollinating. Pods are 1 to 2 inches long. Usually there are two nuts, or seeds per pod, occasionally three. The embryo rests between the two meaty halves of the seed. Seed colors vary from whitish to dark purple but mahogany red, rose and salmon predominate. Each bit of the peanut has a use: the pod or shell, the seed, and the skin. The seeds, or nuts, contain 40-50 percent oil, 20-30 percent protein and 5-15 percent carbohydrates and other things.

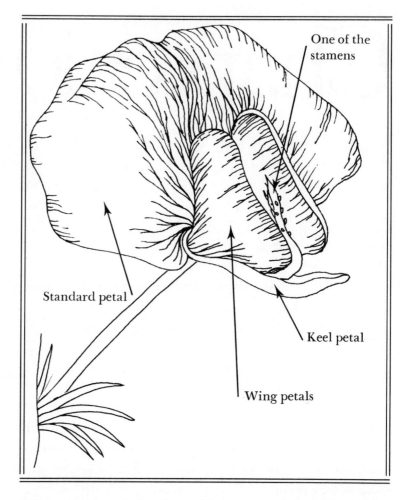

One of the
stamens

Standard petal

Keel petal

Wing petals

The purpose of the flower is to reproduce the species by causing the plant to produce seeds. The peanut flower is self-pollinating. It has both stamens and stigma, the male and female organs needed for reproduction. Self-pollination means that seeds are not produced by the transference of pollen from one flower to another by means of bees and other insects, but are produced by the single flower itself. The peanut flower has one large petal in the back, called the standard petal. It has two side, or wing, petals, and a keel petal. The stamens are inside the wing petals and the stigma is inside the keel petal. The petals of the peanut flower are at the top of a long tube and the ovaries are at the bottom of this tube.

A stalk connects the stigma and ovary inside the tube. Self-pollination occurs when the stamen opens and pollen dusts onto the stigma in the flower. This usually happens in the early morning when the flower itself is still closed. In the next few hours, the pollen grows a tube of its own down to the ovary through the long stalk of the pistil, the ovule-bearing organ. When the pollen tube reaches the ovary, the pollen fertilizes the ovules, and they become seeds. The flower, having fulfilled its purpose, withers and falls off. The fertilized ovary grows slowly and in a few days its increased weight causes it to grow down to the ground.

The stems of your peanut plant support the leaves and flowers and carry water and food from place to place within the plant. The peanut stem is a typical soft, herbaceous, stem. It's branched and leafy. The point at which the leaf joins the stem is called the node. There are several nodes on a stem. The distance between two nodes is an internode. On a Runner peanut plant, the first two nodes on the first lateral branch are fruiting nodes. The next two nodes are vegetative nodes for growing leaves and other branches. It continues that way, alternating two fruiting and two vegetative. Other types of peanuts may bear fruit on the main stem as well as on the lateral branches, and each node close to the soil can bear fruit.

*The Peanut Plant Stem*

# Part 2

# Cooking
and
Eating

# Chapter 1

When your peanuts are dry, there's only one thing left to do. Eat them!

*Raw*  Eat a few raw for that good "goober pea" taste, the very same taste the soldiers in the Civil War grew to love. You don't have to learn to love goobers. Just try one to get a sense of history.

*Roasted*  *In the shell*  Put your raw peanuts one or two layers deep in a shallow baking pan. Roast at 350° for 25 to 30 minutes, occasionally stirring them. During the last few minutes of roasting, taste one to make sure the rest are done the way you like them. The smell of peanuts roasting is terrific.

*Out of the shell*  After you shell your peanuts, take the skins off the nuts. The easiest and best way is by *blanching*. Put your raw peanuts into boiling water. Turn off the heat. Let them stand for about 3 minutes. Drain the water. Slide the skins off with your fingers. They should slide easily. Spread them on paper towels to dry. Now the peanuts can be salted, fried or roasted.

    If you want to roast them, put your raw, blanched, shelled peanuts one layer deep in a shallow baking pan. Bake at 350° for 15 to 20 minutes until golden brown, turning every so often to avoid scorch-

*37.*

ing. To check if they're done, taste one. You can garnish with melted butter, then salt them to your taste. *Don't Throw Away the Shells* Feed them to your houseplants or to your garden. Just crumble them up and work them into the soil. They will enrich it.

## Spicy Toasted Peanuts

1/4 cup water
1 1/2 teaspoons salt
1/4 teaspoon Allspice
1 pound raw peanuts, blanched

Preheat oven to 275°. Heat water. Stir in salt to dissolve, then Allspice. Add raw peanuts and mix well together. Then pour mixture onto a roasting pan and spread out flat. Roast for about an hour until peanuts are a pale golden brown. Stir every 10 minutes for even coloring and flavor. Serve hot or cold.

## Curried Peanuts

1 1/2 teaspoons salt
1/2 teaspoon curry powder
1/4 cup water
1 pound raw peanuts, blanched

Preheat oven to 275°. Dissolve salt and curry powder in heated water. Add raw peanuts and mix well together. Then pour mixture into a roasting pan and spread peanuts out in one layer. Roast for about an hour till peanuts are a pale golden brown. Stir once in a while. Serve hot or cold.

## Glazed Peanuts

1 cup sugar
½ cup water
2 cups raw peanuts with skins

Dissolve sugar in water in a heavy frying pan over medium heat. Add peanuts and continue cooking on medium-high heat, stirring constantly. Cook until the peanuts have a shiny glazed rosy look. Spread onto aluminum foil to cool. Break apart while still warm. After cooling, store in airtight container.

## French Fried Peanuts

Using peanut oil, cook raw, blanched peanuts in a layer of oil that's deep enough to cover the peanuts. First heat oil to 300°, then add the peanuts. Stir occasionally. When peanuts begin to brown, take them out of the oil as they'll continue to brown while cooling. Drain peanuts. Spread on brown paper for further draining. Salt right away to taste. Use fine ground salt for best results.

## Garlic Peanuts

Put a clove of garlic into a jar with a cup of peanuts. Cover the jar tightly and keep it in the refrigerator for a few hours.

*Some Quick and Easy Things to Do with Roasted and Salted Peanuts*

## Peanuts and Ice Cream

Drop some peanuts on top of your favorite flavor ice cream. If you use vanilla ice cream and chocolate topping, it's a "tin-roof" sundae.

## Peanuts and Coleslaw

Add chopped peanuts and diced unpeeled red apples to coleslaw!

*Peanuts and Egg Salad*

Add chopped peanuts to your favorite egg salad.

*Peanut Casserole Topping*

Combine ¼ cup chopped peanuts with ¼ cup bread crumbs and 2 tablespoons peanut oil and use as a topping for your favorite casserole.

*Peanut Stew Topping*

Sprinkle on top of beef stew or lamb stew.

*Peanuts and Gazpacho*

Toss some chopped peanuts into gazpacho or other cold soups.

*Peanut Munch*

Mix together 1 cup of peanuts with some sunflower seeds, some golden raisins and currants.

*Peanuts and Celery and Cream Cheese*

Mix some chopped peanuts with a packet of cream cheese. Spread the mixture in the hollow of celery sticks. Serve as hors d'oeuvres.

*Peanuts and Green Beans*

Add some chopped peanuts and butter to hot green beans, spinach, or squash for a crunchy texture.

*Peanuts and Salad*

Toss a few chopped peanuts into your favorite salad.

*Peanuts and Chutney*

Add chopped peanuts to your favorite chutney.

It's the ultimate. There's nothing else quite like it. *Homemade*
And making it yourself is cheaper than buying it in a *Peanut*
store. You'll need an electric blender, peanuts roasted *Butter*
to your taste, some peanut oil. If you leave the skins
on your peanuts, they'll add a nice texture. It's okay
to take them off, too.

Many people prefer not to use any oil in their
homemade peanut butter. Depending on your blender,
you may need a touch to help in the blending process.
And if you like a more spreadable consistency, you'll
probably want to add oil. Figure on using 1 tablespoon
to 1 cup of peanuts. You can experiment with less or
more oil till you get it to your taste.

Put your cup of peanuts, with or without oil,
into your blender and mix until it's smooth enough for
you. Add salt to taste. That's it. For chunky peanut
butter, add a few chopped peanuts to the mixture and
mix them in by hand. You could add honey, sesame
seeds, raisins, curry powder, orange bits, bananas, bean
sprouts, or, of course, old reliable jelly. Homemade
peanut butter separates fairly quickly. The oil rises
to the top. Just stir it before using.

The very first peanut butter creation to achieve
fame was concocted in 1890, by a St. Louis physician
whose name has been lost to us. He wanted to make an
easily digestible and eatable high protein diet for his
geriatric patients. Today, most peanut butter sandwiches are wolfed down by kids, four to twelve. Most,
but not all. Half of all the peanuts raised in this country are used to make peanut butter! Adult peanut
butter cultists exist everywhere. There are those who
eat it chunky, while others take it smooth. Then there
is the cold-from-the-refrigerator group never to be con-

fused with the room-temperature gang. And they are all surprisingly particular about the ways they eat their peanut butter. Some scoff at the idea of bread, some sneer at the mention of jelly, some purists eat it straight from the jar. Here's a small sampling of how peanut butter fans eat their peanut butter:

*A Peanut Butter Maven:* "I get my jar of homemade peanut butter and a spoon. I take the lid off the jar and grasp it firmly in my left hand. I take a spoon in my right hand. With a relaxed, digging motion I scoop the peanut butter out of the jar and into my mouth. I keep scooping and eating until I've had enough. Then I label the jar with my name in black magic marker. I never use bread. It's a waste and fattening anyhow."

*A Midnight Sensualist:* "The most incredible experience is peanut butter and almond butter. (Sigh) On anything. (Sigh) Bread, crackers, it doesn't matter. If nothing's around, first I eat a spoonful of peanut butter and then a spoonful of almond butter. (Pause) It's wonderful. The best time to have it is at midnight . . . with a glass of milk. (Sigh)"

*Sweet Tooth:* "I like chunky peanut butter on plain white bread with marshmallow fluff. Though, since I've grown up, I sometimes eat jelly instead of fluff."

*A Touchy Eater:* "I adore my peanut butter straight from the jar. With my finger, not a knife. When I have it on bread, I like it warm out of the cupboard because when it's cold it rips my bread."

*A No-Nonsense Type:* "I eat peanut butter on whole wheat bread for lunch almost every day with a glass of milk. No jelly. No nothing. Absolutely plain."

*A Texture Expert:* "First I get the heel slice of whole wheat bread. I spread chunky peanut butter on the whole thing, end to end, then spread orange marmalade on just half of it. Then I fold the bread over like a hot dog roll and slowly bite through all the different textures. Hmmm."

*A Comic:* "What do I eat my peanut butter on? I put a spoonful of peanut butter in my mouth. Then I eat it off the roof of my mouth."

*A Peanut Butter Freak:* "I love peanut butter best on toasted whole wheat English muffins. I leave the jar out for awhile so it warms up because I hate it when it's cold. I learned early in life that it's very very important to always eat a peanut butter and jelly sandwich with the jelly side up so the peanut butter won't stick to the roof of your mouth."

*A Gourmet Snob:* "I prefer my peanut butter in the hollow of a half of a perfectly ripe avocado."

# Chapter 2

*Snacks*

## A Peanut Shake

1 small banana
¼ cup smooth peanut butter
½ pint vanilla ice cream
1 cup milk

In a blender, or mixing bowl, blend banana until smooth. Blend in peanut butter and then ice cream. Add milk and beat until smooth. *Serves 2.*

## Nippy Peanut Spread

1 cup peanuts, salted and chopped
1 cup soft sharp cheese, grated
½ cup softened butter
⅔ cup olives, finely chopped
dash pepper
dash Worcestershire sauce

Combine all ingredients and mix to blend. Serve on your favorite crackers. *Makes over 3 cups.*

## Peanut Butter and Cheese Soup

2 tablespoons butter
2 tablespoons flour
4 cups milk
½ cup leeks, finely chopped
2½ tablespoons sharp cheddar cheese, grated
¼ teaspoon celery seed
¼ teaspoon black pepper
⅓ cup peanut butter
1 bay leaf
*Garnish:* bacon bits or roasted Spanish peanuts

Melt the butter and mix it in with the flour. Add milk and the rest of the ingredients. Bring to a boil. Simmer 15 minutes. Take out bay leaf. Garnish. Serve hot or cold. *Serves 4.*

## Tuskegee Soup

4 or 5 scallions, diced
½ cup peanut butter
3 tablespoons cornstarch
2 cups chicken stock
½ cup cream
juice from 1 quart of oysters
salt
cayenne
summer savory
2 to 3 tablespoons sherry
1 quart oysters, drained
*Garnish:* chopped parsley

Sauté scallions for 2 minutes. Stir in the peanut butter and cornstarch, blending until smooth. Take mixture off heat. Stir in chicken stock. Return to heat until mixture thickens. Add cream and oyster juice. Season with salt, cayenne, summer savory, and sherry. Add oysters and heat to serving temperature. Garnish. This soup was brewed in many colonial kitchens. *Serves 4.*

*Peanut-Banana Salad*

2 tablespoons smooth peanut butter
1½ teaspoons orange peel, grated
1½ teaspoons crystalline ginger, finely chopped
2 small bananas, split lengthwise
¼ cup mayonnaise
1 tablespoon orange juice
½ to ¾ cup peanuts, chopped
fresh fruits in season
lettuce
"Creamy Orange Dressing"

Combine peanut butter, orange peel, and ginger. Spread 1 tablespoon mixture on two of the banana halves and top each with remaining split bananas. Cut each into 4 pieces and dip into a combination of the mayonnaise and orange juice. Roll in chopped peanuts to coat. Serve with fresh fruit on lettuce. Top with "Creamy Orange Dressing." *Serves 8.*

*Creamy Orange Dressing:* In a small bowl combine ½ cup evaporated milk, ½ cup smooth peanut butter, 1 tablespoon grated orange peel, and ¼ cup orange juice. Chill. *Makes 1⅓ cups.*

*Peanut Health Salad*

½ cup peanuts, salted and chopped
½ cup dates, chopped
2 cups cottage cheese
lettuce
*Garnish:* watercress

Mix peanuts and dates together. Arrange cottage cheese on a bed of lettuce. Spoon peanut and date mixture onto each serving. Garnish. *Serves 2.*

In parts of the world, peanuts, peanut butter, and peanut oil are important day-to-day ingredients in cooking. French chefs prefer peanut oil to any other kind of vegetable oil because it doesn't smoke at high temperatures. In the regions of Africa where peanuts are grown, Senegal and Nigeria, the natives grind peanuts in a mortar and pestle and pound them into a paste. This paste is sometimes eaten with rice, but most of it goes into the dish cooked that day. Peanuts are part of the daily lives of people of peanut-growing regions in India and mainland China. Here are some recipes for main courses using peanuts, from all around the world.

*Ugandan Peanut Butter Stew*

3 tablespoons oil
2 onions, chopped
4 cloves garlic, pressed
2 carrots, diced
1 cauliflower, cut into small pieces
6 to 8 tomatoes, sliced; or 1 can (1 pound) tomatoes,
      including the liquid
$\frac{1}{2}$ cup peanut butter
$\frac{1}{2}$ cup water
$\frac{1}{2}$ teaspoon chili powder
1 teaspoon cayenne pepper
salt to taste

Heat the oil in a skillet and sauté the onions and garlic. Add the carrots and cauliflower and continue to cook. After 2 or 3 minutes, add the tomatoes, cover, lower the heat, and simmer for 30 minutes. Then add the peanut butter, water, and seasonings. Cook 5 to 10 minutes more. Serve with brown rice. *Serves 4.*

## Chinese Chicken and Peanuts

1 tablespoon brown bean sauce
2 tablespoons water
2 tablespoons cornstarch
1/2 teaspoon cayenne pepper
1/2 teaspoon mushroom soy sauce
2 to 3 tablespoons peanut oil
2 or 3 slices fresh ginger root, finely chopped
1/2 chicken, skinned, boned, and diced
1 1/4 tablespoons sherry
5 dried black mushrooms, soaked and diced
3 scallion stalks, cut into 1/2-inch pieces
1/2 cup unsalted peanuts

In one cup, mash the brown bean sauce and mix with 1 tablespoon water. In another cup, mix cornstarch and the rest of the water, stirring in cayenne pepper and mushroom soy. Heat the oil. Add the ingredients to the frying pan, always remembering to stir while they are cooking. First, add the ginger root. Fry and stir for 1 minute. Next add the chicken. Fry and stir for 1 minute. Add the sherry. Fry and stir for 1 minute. Add the mushrooms. Fry and stir for 1/2 minute. Add brown bean mixture, scallions, and peanuts. Fry and stir for 1 more minute. Stir in cornstarch to thicken. Serve immediately. For a spicier taste, add more cayenne. *Serves 6.*

## Chinese Pork with Peanuts

1 tablespoon flour
1¼ tablespoons sherry
1½ tablespoons mushroom soy sauce
½ pound lean pork, diced
1½ tablespoons peanut oil
½ cup raw peanuts, salted
2 tablespoons peanut oil
1 garlic clove, crushed
¼ pound fresh mushrooms, diced
2 scallions, diced
½ cup beef stock
*Garnish:* celery ribs, finely chopped

Mix together the flour, sherry, and mushroom soy; then add to the pork. Mix until pork is coated. Heat peanut oil. Add peanuts to oil and brown lightly. Drain on paper towels. Heat rest of oil. Brown garlic. Add pork and keep stirring, about 2 or 3 minutes, until meat loses all pinkness. Add the mushrooms and scallions. Fry about ½ minute until coated with oil. Stir in the stock and heat it quickly. Cover. Cook over medium heat until done, about 4 minutes. Stir in peanuts and reheat. Serve immediately. Garnish. *Serves 4 to 5.*

### Thailand Beef (or Chicken) Satay

1 pound lean beef, cut in 1-inch cubes (chicken
      may be substituted)
peanut oil

*Satay Sauce*
1 tablespoon ground coriander seeds
2 teaspoons ground fennel
2 teaspoons ground cumin
¾ teaspoon chili powder
2 teaspoons shrimp paste
1 clove garlic, finely minced
2 small onions, chopped
2 tablespoons peanut oil
1¼ cups coconut milk*
1¼ teaspoons sherry
1 teaspoon brown sugar
4 to 6 tablespoons peanut butter
salt to taste
lemon juice (1 lemon)

Make the Satay Sauce by combining the coriander, fennel, cumin, and chili powder. Fry with the shrimp paste, garlic, and onions in the peanut oil. Add the coconut milk, sherry, brown sugar, peanut butter, and salt. Simmer 12 minutes and add lemon juice.

Put beef cubes onto skewers. Broil. Baste with peanut oil. Pour Satay Sauce over cubes. Serve with diced cucumbers and brown rice. *Serves 4 to 6.*

\* To make the coconut milk, blend ¾ cup packaged shredded coconut with ¾ cup scalded milk in an electric blender. Let mixture stand for 20 to 25 minutes. Strain. *Makes 1¼–1½ cups.*

*Peanut Cinnamon Bread*

2 cups flour, sifted
3 teaspoons baking powder
1¼ teaspoons salt
⅓ cup sugar
1¼ teaspoon orange bits
¼ teaspoon cinnamon
1 cup peanut butter
2 eggs
1¼ cups milk
¾ cup peanuts, chopped

Mix together the sifted flour, baking powder, salt, and sugar. Add orange bits and cinnamon, and mix thoroughly. Add peanut butter. Combine eggs and milk, and add to dry ingredients. Stir to moisten. Add peanuts and pour mixture into a 9-inch loaf pan. Bake at 350° for 1 hour and 10 minutes. *Makes 1 loaf.*

## Peanut Butter Apple Muffins

2 cups all-purpose flour, sifted
4 teaspoons baking powder
¾ teaspoon salt
½ teaspoon cinnamon
¼ teaspoon nutmeg
¼ cup shortening
¼ cup peanut butter
¼ cup sugar
1 egg
1 cup milk
¾ cup raw apple, chopped
2 tablespoons sugar
¼ teaspoon cinnamon

Sift together flour, baking powder, salt, ½ teaspoon cinnamon, and nutmeg. Cream shortening and peanut butter together thoroughly. Gradually add ¼ cup sugar, beating until light and fluffy. Add egg and beat well. Stir in milk and apple. Add flour mixture, all at once, and stir just enough to moisten dry ingredients. Pour into greased 2-inch diameter muffin tins until ⅔ full. Blend together remaining sugar and cinnamon. Sprinkle on tops of muffin batter. Bake in 400° oven for 20 to 25 minutes. Serve warm. *Makes 15 to 18 muffins.*

*Peanut Pancakes*

2 cups all-purpose baking mix (Bisquick)
1⅓ cups milk
1 egg
1 teaspoon orange peel, grated
½ cup peanuts, chopped
peanut oil
"Peanut Butter Honey Topping"

With a rotary beater, beat together baking mix, milk, egg, and orange peel until smooth. Stir in peanuts. Using a ¼-cup measure, pour batter onto heated griddle brushed with peanut oil. Brown until bubbly and edges are baked. Turn and brown other side. Serve with "Peanut Butter Honey Topping." *Makes about 18 cakes.*

    *Peanut Butter Honey Topping:* Blend ¾ cup honey, ½ cup smooth peanut butter, and ¼ cup fresh orange juice. *Makes 1½ cups.*

*Simplified Peanut Butter Pancakes*

Simply add 3 tablespoons of peanut butter to 1 cup of your favorite pancake mix. Follow the directions for other ingredients on your pancake mix box. Bake on a preheated lightly greased skillet or grill. *Serves 2.*

*Peanut Butter Pound Cake*

1 pound cake
¾ cup peanut butter
¾ cup jelly, or jam
¼ cup lemon juice
1 cup heavy cream, whipped

Cut cake crosswise into three layers. Blend peanut butter, jelly, and lemon juice. Spread between layers. Top cake with whipped cream.

*Southern Peanut Pie*

1 tablespoon flour
¼ cup sugar
1 teaspoon salt
2 tablespoons water
½ cup light syrup
3 eggs
1 tablespoon butter
½ cup raw peanuts
¼ cup shredded coconut
1 9-inch pie crust
1 cup heavy cream, whipped

Combine flour, sugar, and salt. Add water and syrup, and blend together. Boil gently 3 to 5 minutes. Beat eggs slightly. Slowly pour syrup mixture into eggs, stirring continuously. Add butter and stir until melted. Place peanuts and coconut in bottom of pie crust and pour the filling over this. Bake at 425° for 10 minutes, then reduce heat to 350° for 30 minutes. Cool. Serve topped with whipped cream.

*Peanut Butter Soufflé*

1 envelope unflavored gelatin
½ cup brown sugar
3 tablespoons peanut butter
1 cup orange juice concentrate
¼ teaspoon salt
4 egg yolks
½ teaspoon ginger
4 egg whites
½ cup granulated sugar
1 cup heavy cream, whipped
*Garnish:* ¼ cup peanuts or candied fruit

In a saucepan, dissolve the gelatin in 2 tablespoons of warm water. Add the brown sugar, peanut butter, orange juice, salt, and egg yolks, and stir until blended. Cook over low heat, stirring constantly, until the peanut butter is melted. Allow to cool. Add the ginger. Beat the egg whites to soft peaks. Gradually add the granulated sugar until the egg whites are in stiff peaks. Fold the egg whites into the peanut butter mixture.

Whip the cream and fold it in. Wrap a waxed paper collar around a 1½ quart soufflé dish or a round bowl with straight sides so that the collar protrudes 2 inches above the rim. Pour the mixture into the dish, to the top of the collar. Chill until firm. Remove the collar and garnish. *Serves 6 to 8.*

*Peanut Coconut Cookies*

1 cup shortening
1 cup smooth peanut butter
½ cup packed light brown sugar
¾ cup regular sugar
1 egg
1 teaspoon vanilla extract
1¾ cups all-purpose flour
1 teaspoon baking powder
1 teaspoon baking soda
½ teaspoon salt
½ cup flaked coconut

Cream together shortening and peanut butter. Add sugars and beat until light and fluffy. Beat in egg and vanilla. Sift together flour, baking powder, baking soda, and salt. Gradually add to creamed mixture. Fold in coconut. On a lightly floured surface shape into two rolls about 8½ inches long. Wrap in waxed paper and chill thoroughly. Cut into ⅛-inch slices and place on a baking sheet brushed with peanut oil. Bake in a 400° oven for 8 to 10 minutes. Cool on a wire rack. *Makes 4 to 5 dozen cookies.*

## Dixie Peanut Wafers

2 cups all-purpose flour
½ teaspoon baking powder
½ teaspoon salt
½ cup shortening
1 cup sugar
1 teaspoon vanilla
¾ cup milk
1 quart raw peanuts, chopped coarsely

Sift flour, baking powder, and salt together. Cream shortening and sugar. Add vanilla. To this mixture, add dry ingredients alternately with milk. Mix in peanuts. Measure 1 tablespoon for each cookie. Flatten with back of spoon on greased baking sheet. Bake at 350° for 15 minutes, or until lightly browned. *Makes 100 cookies.*

## Sweet Peanut Rolls

½ cup honey
½ cup crunchy peanut butter
½ cup non-fat dry milk

Mix honey and peanut butter in a bowl. Stir in non-fat dry milk, a little at a time, until thoroughly blended. Shape into narrow roll. Wrap in waxed paper and chill until firm. Cut into 1-inch pieces and wrap in cellophane. *Makes about ½ pound.*

*Peanut Butter Cookies with Raw Spanish Peanuts*

½ cup vegetable shortening
½ cup sugar
½ cup smooth peanut butter
½ cup firmly packed brown sugar
1 egg
1¼ cups sifted all-purpose flour
½ teaspoon baking powder
¾ teaspoon baking soda
¼ teaspoon salt
½ cup raw Spanish peanuts, blanched

Mix together first five ingredients. Stir in remaining ingredients. Drop by teaspoonfuls on lightly greased baking sheet. Bake at 375° for 10 to 12 minutes. *Makes about 3 dozen cookies.*

## Chocolate Peanut Crunchies

1 6-ounce package semi-sweet chocolate pieces
1 tablespoon peanut oil
½ cup smooth peanut butter
2 tablespoons confectioners' sugar
75 to 80 miniature shredded wheat biscuits
40 whole peanuts

In a small saucepan over hot water, heat chocolate and oil until melted. Stir in peanut butter and sugar until smooth. Dip each miniature biscuit in peanut mixture to coat and place on waxed paper. Top each with a peanut half. Chill. *Makes 75 to 80 candies.*

## Chocolate Peanut Raisin Clusters

½ pound sweet chocolate, cut into pieces
½ cup raw peanuts
½ cup seedless raisins

Melt chocolate. Cool slightly. Add peanuts and raisins and mix well. Drop mixture by spoonfuls on baking sheets covered with waxed paper. Chill until set. *Makes ¾ pound.*

*Peanut Caramel Puffs*

2 14-ounce packages caramels
1/4 cup water
1 10-ounce package marshmallows
4 cups roasted peanuts, chopped

Melt caramels and water over low heat, stirring occasionally until smooth. Dip marshmallows into caramel syrup, using a fork and coating them completely. Roll in chopped peanuts. Place on waxed paper and let dry at room temperature. If caramel thickens, add 1 teaspoon boiling water and stir until smooth. When firm, store candies in an airtight container until ready to serve. *Makes approximately 20 pieces.*

*Peanut Chocolate Fudge*

2 squares unsweetened chocolate
2 cups sugar
⅔ cup milk
2 tablespoons corn syrup
½ teaspoon salt
2 tablespoons butter
¼ cup peanut butter
1 teaspoon vanilla
½ cup roasted peanuts, chopped

Combine chocolate, sugar, milk, corn syrup, and salt together in a saucepan. Heat to 236° F. on a candy thermometer or until a little syrup forms a soft ball in cold water. Stir occasionally to prevent sticking. Remove saucepan from range and place in cold water. Add butter and peanut butter. Let mixture cool to lukewarm without stirring. Add vanilla. Beat until mixture loses its gloss. Quickly add chopped peanuts. Pour into an 8 x 8-inch buttered pan. Cool before cutting. *Makes about 4 dozen pieces.*

*Peanut Brittle*

1 cup water
2½ cups sugar
1 cup white corn syrup
3 cups unroasted unsalted raw shelled peanuts
1 teaspoon salt
2 tablespoons butter
½ teaspoon baking soda
1 teaspoon vanilla
1 pair clean white cotton gloves
1 candy thermometer

Boil water in a heavy 4-quart pan. Stir in sugar until it dissolves. Add the corn syrup, nuts, and salt. Stir. Keep stirring to make sure the peanuts cook and the candy mixture doesn't burn. Stir until the candy thermometer reaches 295°. Remove from heat. Immediately stir in butter, baking soda, and vanilla. The candy will foam up. Remove from heat and pour onto a buttered slab or counter top. Quickly spread the mixture with a spatula. Use the cotton gloves to handle the candy. With a scraper, loosen the candy from the slab. Flip the candy over. Put scraper down. With your gloved hands, stretch and pull the brittle until it gets so thin you can see through it. Cool. Crack into pieces. Peanut brittle tends to get moist so store in a tightly covered tin.

*Peanut Brownies*

4 ounces unsweetened chocolate
½ cup butter
2 cups sugar
3 eggs
1 teaspoon vanilla
1 cup sifted all-purpose flour
½ teaspoon salt
1 cup peanuts

Melt the chocolate and butter in a double boiler. Remove from the heat. Stir well and then stir in the sugar and beat in the eggs and vanilla. Quickly stir in the flour and salt. Add peanuts. Spread into a well greased 9 x 13-inch baking pan. Bake at 325° for 25 minutes. Cool. Cut into squares. *Makes about 30 pieces.*

# Part 3

# Fun and Games

# Chapter 1

Peanuts originated more than 5000 years ago in Peru. That makes them one of the world's oldest foods. Early records tell how they grew along the Maranon River. Peanut designs and shapes constantly show up on ancient Peruvian pottery. In Incan and pre-Incan times, real peanuts were put in graves to give a mummy sustenance on his or her way to heaven. And during recent excavations of these graves, the peanuts, kept in carefully sealed containers, were found to be perfectly preserved even after thousands of years.

Back in the sixteenth century, the Spanish conquistadors sailed to South America to find gold. Instead, they found peanuts. They must have eaten a lot of peanuts in Peru while searching for gold, because they decided they couldn't live without them. When they sailed back to Spain and Portugal, peanuts went with them to the homeland. The peanuts flourished there and became a very important crop.

Before too long, Spain and Portugal began to freight peanuts to Africa on trading ships in exchange for spices and elephant tusks. It was in Angola that peanuts got their nickname "goober" from the Kimbundu word "nguba."

Besides eating peanuts, Africans worshiped them because they believed that peanuts, along with some other species of plant life, had souls. And legend has it that in those regions of Africa where gold was produced, native craftsmen hammered the crude ore into the shape of peanuts. These golden peanut nuggets were presented as trophies to champion warriors, athletes, and hunters. Tribal chiefs made the presentations at great festivals and feasts. The Golden Peanut was a coveted award. This legend was told to Americans by Africans brought here in Spanish trading ships and sold in Virginia as slaves.

Also in the gold-producing sections of Africa, casts of peanuts were made, coated with bronze or brass and used as weights to weigh the gold on scales. Other things from nature, like insects, were used as weights, too. Some had proverbs or special meanings connected to them. When one tribal chief wanted to say something to another tribal chief, he sent whatever weight had the appropriate message he wanted to convey. Unfortunately, the meanings of many of these weights, including the peanut, were not recorded. So we'll never know what message the bronzed peanut carried.

When the African slave ships came to this country, peanuts came with them. They came as a favored food for the long voyage and as reassuring symbols of native lore, culture, and beliefs. Some peanuts from the slave ships ended up in American ground. The first peanuts to be planted here were in Virginia at the slave quarters on the fringes of the large plantations. They were carefully cultivated as part of sacred African tradition.

Most of the early peanuts were grown in Virginia, some in other parts of the South, all mainly for local consumption. Early Americans didn't take to peanuts right away.

Then the Civil War came. Union and Confederate soldiers alike enjoyed eating raw peanuts, or "goober peas," fresh from the peanut fields. They even sang a song about them.

Goober Peas

Sitting by the roadside on a summer day,
Chatting with my mess-mates, passing time away,
Lying in the shadow underneath the trees,
Goodness, how delicious, eating goober peas!

Chorus:
Peas! Peas! Peas! Peas! Eating goober peas!
Goodness, how delicious, eating goober peas!

When a horseman passes the soldiers have a rule,
To cry out at their loudest, "Mister, where's your
        mule?"
But another pleasure enchantinger than these,
Is wearing out your grinders, eating goober peas!

Chorus.

Just before the battle, the General hears a row,
He says, "The Yanks are coming, I hear their rifles
        now."
He turns around in wonder, and what do you think he
        sees?
The Georgia Militia, eating goober peas!

Chorus.

I think my song has landed almost long enough.
The subject's interesting, but the rhymes are rough;
I wish this war was over, when free from rags and fleas,
We'd kiss our wives and sweethearts, and gobble goober
        peas.

Chorus.

When the war was over, and the Union soldiers went back North, they missed and craved the peanuts. A demand for peanuts started. Confederates brought pocketfuls of peanuts back to their scattered homes. And the planting of peanuts throughout the rest of the South began to spread.

When the circus wagons rolled into town, they brought animals, lion tamers, clowns, tight-rope walkers, the daring young men on the flying trapeze, and peanuts! As peanuts were introduced to more parts of the country, our collective peanut craving started to grow. The peanut industry recognizes its debt to the circus. In fact, in 1952 when Cecil B. DeMille produced his Oscar-winning motion picture, *The Greatest Show on Earth,* the peanut industry presented him with the first Golden Peanut ever given to anyone in this country.

When baseball started becoming a national obsession, stadiums all over the country sold hot roasted peanuts by the bagful. Rowdy, hungry, cheering fans ate peanuts and got more energy to be rowdy, hungry and cheering. We all know this song.

| | |
|---|---|
| Take Me Out to the Ball Game (1908) | Take me out to the ball game<br>Take me out with the crowds<br>Buy me some peanuts and crackerjacks<br>I don't care if I ever get back!<br><br>Let me root root root for the home team<br>If they don't win it's a shame<br>For it's one, two, three strikes you're out<br>At the old ball game! |

Peanuts and baseball are now so inseparable that just a few years ago when a baseball club owner threatened to keep them out of his ball park, the fans wouldn't stand for it. Paul I. Fagan, the owner of the San Francisco Seals announced, at the end of one season, there would be no more roasted peanuts in his ball park because it cost too much to sweep the shells out after every game. The raging protests of the fans were so awesome, Fagan not only took back his order, but gave out free peanuts at the next season's opening game. Just last year, at Dodgers' games alone, 1,800,000 bags of peanuts were sold.

The Civil War, the circus, and baseball all get credit for the proliferation of the peanut because they continued to spark appetites in the North, East, and West. The spread of peanuts also gained momentum when the boll weevil wiped out most of the southern cotton crops in the years following the Civil War. A wizard of a botanist by the name of George Washington Carver (1864-1943) traveled relentlessly from farm to farm in the 1890's talking up the virtues of peanuts. He started a personal campaign to convince Alabama farmers to try growing peanuts in soil all worn out by cotton. He knew peanuts could put new life into tired soil. And the cotton crop itself was being increasingly ruined by the boll weevil. The South needed peanuts. But to convince farmers wasn't easy. Their attitudes towards peanuts were scornful. Just nonsense "circus chaw" with no food value at all was what they thought of peanuts. But once Carver managed to get farmers enthused about growing peanuts, he put himself to the task of finding uses for them. Did he ever. How about peanut lemon punch, peanut orange punch, and cheese. He got 35 pounds of cheese from 100 pounds of peanut milk. The same amount of cow's milk yields 8 to 10 pounds of cheese. Peanut ink, axle grease, gasoline, a dandruff treatment, glue, bleach, washing powder, ointments, linoleum, even rubber, to name a few. Carver even made a linen-like paper from peanut skins and yucca stalks to save the Southland's spruce trees. He never sought any pay for any of his inventions. Before he died, he was able to see that the peanut had finally made it here.

Today, in the town square of Enterprise, Alabama, sits a monument to the boll weevil. Local farmers put it there. When they realized more money could be made from peanuts than from cotton, they agreed the coming of the boll weevil was a boon, not a blight. Peanuts not only solved their economic problems but also, true to Carver's word, revitalized the tired soil. It seems peanuts have a special talent for putting nitrogen back into the soil instead of taking it out.

Today, there are 84,000 peanut farmers in the major peanut-producing states of Georgia, Texas, Alabama, North Carolina, Oklahoma, Virginia, Florida, New Mexico, and Mississippi. Altogether, 1.5 million acres yield about 3.5 billion pounds of peanuts each year with a farm value exceeding $800 million annually. Peanuts rank among our top ten crops. That's only about 8 percent of the entire world's peanut production. We eat more than half the peanuts we grow while the rest of the world uses its peanuts mainly for edible oils. Peanuts have come a long way since the mummies.

# Chapter 2

They seem to be endless. Every part of the peanut, the shell, the nut, the heart; that small nugget between the two halves where germination starts, even the plant itself, has a use. Mostly, we eat them. In peanut butter: smooth, chunky, dietetic, with honey, with cheddar cheese, with wheat germ. Some end up roasted, salted, and in peanut candies: brittles, nut rolls, bars, chocolate covered, butter cups, clusters, fudge, taffy, nougats, crunches, chews, kisses. Not to mention the ubiquitous peanut cracker sandwiches, peanut cookies, cakes and wafers found in vending machines, drugstores, candy counters everywhere. How about flour, cooking and salad oils, mayonnaise. The tops of peanut plants are a savory hay eaten by livestock down South. Once peanuts are crushed for oil, what's left is used as animal feed. Some are used for seed to grow more peanuts.

*Some
Peanut
Uses*

Peanuts we don't eat are used in shaving creams, adhesives, paper, plastics, salve, cosmetics, shampoo, shoe polish, dyes (for cloth, leather, and wood stains), lubricating oils, metal polish, fertilizer, to name a few.

Even the shells of peanuts are used as sound insulation, floor sweeping compound, wall board, mulch for growing plants, roughage for cattle feed when mixed with molasses, litter for poultry houses, abrasives for polishing steel and aluminum, the cork-like stuff on the insides of bottle caps and in compressed form as fireplace logs.

| | |
|---|---|
| *Peanut*<br>*Nutrition* | The peanut is packed with protein, essential B vitamins, minerals—more of all of these than in beef liver—and a balanced share of calories. Peanuts are terrific for growing kids. They have the amino acids needed by growing tissues and niacin to build a steady nervous system. From 4 tablespoons of peanut butter a child can get as much as 40 percent of his daily protein needs. Two peanut butter sandwiches, a glass of milk, and an orange make a perfectly balanced meal. |
| *Peanut*<br>*Dreams* | In dreams, peanuts are considered a fortunate omen unless they're wormy or stale in which case they forewarn problems arising from direct or hostile competition. Cracking peanuts prophesizes success. Eating peanuts promises good health. Empty nutshells portend futile efforts. |
| *Peanut*<br>*Talk* | The word "peanut" itself has a few different meanings. Smallness, insignificance; a pugnosed person; a football; small change, small salary, the color of flax. |

In colloquial use, its slant is almost always pejorative. Phrases like "peanut head," "for peanuts," "not worth a peanut," all have a familiar ring. The unfamiliar phrase, "to hull the goobers for," means to vanquish, to defeat. "Peanut gallery" refers to the top rows in a theater. Peanut policy is procedure based on low or underhanded methods. Peanut politics are petty or corrupt politics. A peanut roaster is a small locomotive. A peanut wagon is a jalopy that does not qualify as a hot rod. The phrase, "he's got peanut butter in his ears," is "CB" talk for not listening. And to be peanutbrained is to be just plain dumb.

Hubert Humphrey's favorite sandwich is peanut but- *Peanuts* ter, baloney, cheddar cheese, lettuce, and mayonnaise *and* on toasted bread with ketchup on the side. At least *People* it was in 1972. His second favorite is a toasted peanut butter, cheese, and bacon sandwich.

Barry Goldwater once shaved with peanut butter on a dare. Said it was "darn good shaving cream." He prefers the smooth to the chunky.

Chris Ambrose holds the peanut-eating record. 100 peanuts eaten in 59.2 seconds in Clerkenwell, London, on April 3, 1973. And that included shelling.

A South African headmistress has banned peanuts and peanut butter from her school because she thinks they are sexually stimulating.

Edgar Cayce, the psychic, recommends massaging the body with peanut oil twice a week in the treatment of ailments such as arthritis, apoplexy, menopause, poor circulation, and fatigue.

Will Rogers said, in his autobiography, "Course we don't get meat as often as our forefathers. But we have our peanut butter and radio."

Al Geiberger, professional golfer, carries his own personal supply of peanut butter sandwiches with him on the tour.

George Washington Carver used to tell this story. "When I was young I said to God, 'God, tell me the mystery of the universe.' But God answered, 'That knowledge is reserved for me alone.' So I said, 'God, tell me the mystery of the peanut.' Then God said, 'Well, George, that's more nearly your size.' "

Billy Rose, during one of the low spots in his career, was so broke he had only fifteen cents to live on for three days. Billy says, "I simply bought three five-cent bags of peanuts and ate one each day. And, do you know something, I made out just fine."

Helen Hayes met her late husband, playwright Charles MacArthur, when he passed her a small dish of salted peanuts at a party and said, "I wish they were emeralds." They married. Years later, when Charles returned from a trip abroad, he gave her a small bag of emeralds and said, "Do you know something, Helen, I sort of wish they were peanuts."

Lawmakers in the state of Massachusetts demand that peanuts must not be eaten in court. And in the Chicago *Sun Times,* January 5, 1949, we find out "In Massachusetts it's against the law to eat peanuts in church."

Francis G. Benedict in *The Energy Requirements of Intense Mental Effort* tells us, "The extra calories needed for an hour of intense mental effort would be completely met by the eating of one oyster cracker or one half of a salted peanut."

Queen Victoria of England had a standing order that went from the palace to America each week for six Virginia hams, known as Smithfield hams. The hams got their special flavoring, which so appealed to the queen, from all the peanuts they consumed when they were still alive down on the farms in Virginia.

# Chapter 3

Make a collection of peanut people by painting faces
on them. Make peanut necklaces, bracelets, earrings,
rings by painting peanut shells with your favorite colors
and then lacquering them. Instead of stringing popcorn
on your next Christmas tree, try stringing peanuts
instead. Play the game of "Find the Peanut." There
aren't any rules yet so you'll have to make them up.
Or how about a new version of an old party favorite,
"Pin the Shell on the Peanut." Or guess the number of
peanuts in a jar.

Try chanting peanut nursery rhymes to your
peanut plant. But if they make it wilt, you'd better
stop.

Hot roasted peanuts
Tell the teacher she's nuts
If she asks you what's your name
Tell the teacher she's a pain

or

A peanut sat on a railroad track
Its heart was all a flutter
Along came the 5:15
Toot-toot peanut butter.

If you eat your peanuts by cracking the shell neatly in half lengthwise, here's what you can do. With some cardboard and some glue, you can write your name with peanut shells.

Look on the backs of Planters peanut packages for the most current premiums. Most recently, they include a Mr. Peanut Coloring Book, a Mr. Peanut rag doll, Mr. Peanut Pants, a Mr. Peanut Beach Ball, and a Mr. Peanut Bank. If you'd like more information on what's available now and how many empty Planters packets you'll need, write to: Planters, c/o Mr. Peanut, PC-4, Wilkes-Barre, Pa. 18701.

*March Is National Peanut Month*

In 1974, National Peanut Week was expanded to National Peanut Month. You might go to the zoo, celebrate with an elephant and tell him some jokes.

How can you spot a drunken elephant?
By the smell of peanut butter on his breath.

How can you tell if an elephant's been in your refrigerator?
By the footprints in the peanut butter.

Found a peanut, found a peanut,
Found a peanut just now.
Just now I found a peanut
Found a peanut just now.

Cracked it open, cracked it open,
Cracked it open just now.
Just now I cracked it open
Cracked it open just now.

Found it rotten, found it rotten,
Found it rotten just now.
Just now I found it rotten
Found it rotten just now.

Ate it anyhow, ate it anyhow,
Ate it anyhow just now.
Just now I ate it anyhow
Ate it anyhow just now.

Got a tummy ache, got a tummy ache,
Got a tummy ache just now.
Just now I got a tummy ache
Got a tummy ache just now.

Called a doctor, called a doctor,
Called a doctor just now.
Just now I called a doctor
Called a doctor just now.

I died anyway, I died anyway,
I died anyway just now.
Just now I died anyway
I died anyway just now.

Went to heaven, went to heaven,
Went to heaven just now.
Just now I went to heaven
Went to heaven just now.

Found another peanut, found another peanut,
Found another peanut just now.
Just now I found another peanut
Found another peanut just now. . . .

# Index